Flying!

Spying!

Hiding!

Disguising!

And
sapling supplying!

For Vaso and Nikos – T. M.
For Bob x – H.S.

OXFORD
UNIVERSITY PRESS

Great Clarendon Street, Oxford OX2 6DP
Oxford University Press is a department of the University of Oxford.
It furthers the University's objective of excellence in research, scholarship,
and education by publishing worldwide. Oxford is a registered trade mark of
Oxford University Press in the UK and in certain other countries

ISBN: 978-0-19-274679-5

1 3 5 7 9 10 8 6 4 2

Printed in China

Paper used in the production of this book is a natural,
recyclable product made from wood grown in sustainable forests.
The manufacturing process conforms to the environmental
regulations of the country of origin.

Photographs p154 (top) © Peter Turner Photography/Shutterstock,
p154 (bottom) © Ermi/Shutterstock, p156 © Leah Joy Kelton/Shutterstock.

THE NEW ADVENTURES OF MR TOAD

Operation Toad!

Tom Moorhouse

with pictures by Holly Swain

OXFORD
UNIVERSITY PRESS

Contents

Application for your licence to paraglide.

Please complete all the boxes.

(More bits from Teejay to help!)

Mr T's going to fly! That's good, because he's not allowed to drive any more.

Name: Mr Toad, gentle~~man~~ Toad aviator and adventurer.

Address: Toad Hall of course!

Mr Toad

Please give the names of three referees who can tell us about your flying ability. Give details of their qualifications:

Ooh, I'm a referee! Can I have a whistle? And those red and yellow cards?

I'm NOT an aeronaut, you take that back! (What's an aeronaut?)

1) Toad Junior: A fine young Toad and fearless aeronaut. Excellent communications and adventuring skills.

Ratty doesn't want to be a pilot. He only likes boats.

2) Ratty: A water rat. Not pilot material, but excellent at ground repairs, equipment provision and so on. Handy chap with a spanner.

3) Mo: Navigation and flight-planning boffin. Technical wizard and first class mole.

Mo had a cold last week. He was a coughing boffin. Hehehee.

Teejay, Ratty, and Mo

Please provide the name of somebody who can give a character reference:

Ms Badger: This fine lady can tell you what a stable and reliable fellow I am. She is my mentor and guide.

Badge says he's a nightmare. She says if it wasn't for her list he'd be in prison or something.

The list is stuff she won't let Mr T do. Last week she added pogo-sticks, duck racing, and paintball. (Because Mr T made up a game called Pogoducksplat. The ducks were really annoyed.)

Please tell us your reasons for wishing to paraglide:

Two excellent reasons! First, for the benefit of society, I intend to aerially document the recent renovation of Toad Hall's architectural magnificence.

Second, I shall use my powers of flight to keep an eagle eye on the villainous weasels at Wildwood Industrious – particularly the Chief Weasel and his assistant, Mr Ripton.

He's taking pictures of his house now it's fixed.

Badge says the weasels have been quiet, and that spells trubble. I can't spell trubble.

The Chief weasel and Mr Ripton

Mr Polecat's lesson droned on. Teejay put her chin in her hand and wrote: *bored, boredy, bored* in her exercise book. Lennie, at the next desk, giggled. She leant over and wrote: *me too.*

'*Yeeeaaaarrgh!*'

'What?' Teejay whispered.

'I didn't say anything,' said Lennie.

'Oh, I thought I heard a—'

'*Yeaaaaar-aaarrgh!*'

Lennie blinked. 'I heard something too. It's outside!'

'*Nononononono! No! No! Aaarrrghh!*'

They stared out of the window. An object hurtled past, high in the sky. It sped away over the school fields.

'What was that?' Teejay whispered.

'I don't know. Maybe a kite?'

It wheeled around, heading back towards the school. And now Teejay saw a tiny figure dangling beneath it.

'Ooh, it's a parachute or something,' said Teejay.

Lennie pointed. 'And it's getting lower!'

The object dived. It swooped towards them. Below it the tiny figure waggled its arms and legs. It yelled something then zoomed over their heads.

Teejay frowned. 'Did that sound like screaming to you?'

Mr Polecat's paws rapped the desk in front of them. Teejay and Lennie jumped. 'Toad Junior, pay attention!' He frowned at them. 'You too, Lenora Weasel.'

'But we *were* paying attention, Mr Polecat,' said Lennie.

'Not to me you weren't. What was I just saying?'

Lennie swallowed. 'Um, something about Wild Wood?'

Teejay glanced desperately back at Ratty and Mo, sitting behind them. Mo scribbled on a piece of paper, and held it up. It said:

13

Plants-
danger-
protect

'That's it!' said
Teejay. 'We need protecting
from Wild Wood's dangerous plants.'

Mr Polecat sighed. 'No. What I *actually*
said was the Wild Wood's endangered plants
need protecting. Now what's so important out
there?'

'There's a flying thing,' said Teejay.

'A "flying thing", eh? Well of course there
is.' Mr Polecat folded his arms. '*I* can't see a—'

'*Yeeeaaarrrrggghhhh!*'

The flying object shot right over the
classroom roof. It raced off over the fields.

'My word! That's a paraglider!' said Mr
Polecat. 'But what's the pilot playing at?'

Everyone rushed to the windows. Ratty and
Mo crowded in next to Teejay and Lennie.

'Look, it's turning around!' said Ratty.

The pilot pulled on a rope and the paraglider

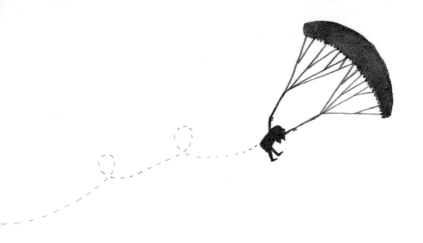

raced in a curve. The curve became a circle, hurtling around again and again, right above the school pond.

Mo pressed his nose to the window. 'Um, I think I know who that is.'

Teejay squinted at the pilot's tweed suit, crash helmet, and flying goggles.

'Yep, that's him all right,' said Ratty.

'Him who?' said Lennie.

'Mr Toad,' Teejay grinned. 'He always wanted to fly!'

Mr Toad struggled with the controls. He kicked his feet and hauled on ropes. But the paraglider's circles got smaller and smaller. And it spun faster and faster, out of control.

'Did he want to crash?' said Ratty. 'Because I think he's going to!'

Chapter 2
Toad fishing

The paraglider whirled. Mr Toad's legs flew up into the air. His shoes shot off his feet.

'This is bad!' Mo whimpered. He ducked below the window.

'Aaaaaaaaaaaaaaaaaaaaaaaaaaaaaaaaaaaaaaaaarrrrrrrrrrrrrrgggggggggggggggghhhhhhhhh!' yelled Mr Toad.

'Come on, Mr T, *do something!*' cried Teejay.

Mr Toad grabbed the control ropes. He gave one final, enormous heave—and the paraglider stopped dead in the air. It seemed to hang, motionless.

17

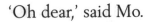

'Oh dear,' said Mo.

The wing folded up, and Mr Toad fell like a rock.

'Noooooooooooooo!'

Sploosh!

He disappeared in a jet of muddy water.

'He's in the pond. He might need help!' cried Teejay. She dashed for the door.

Mr Polecat shouted, 'Toad Junior, come back here!'

But Teejay was already racing down the corridor, Ratty and Mo just behind. They burst onto the playing field and sprinted for the pond. The paraglider's wing covered the water. Except for a Mr Toad-shaped bulge right in the middle.

18

'He's under the parachute thing,' cried Teejay.

'Confound you, you material menace!' Mr Toad's voice was muffled. The bulge seemed to be jumping up and down. 'I shall not tolerate such clothy insubordination!'

'Sounds like he's OK, though,' said Ratty.

'Let's get it off him.' Teejay ran to the bank and grabbed handfuls of the paraglider. 'Take hold everyone,' she shouted. 'Now pull!'

They dragged the wing clear.

'Haha!' called Mr Toad. 'I'm free! I'm free! I'm—'

The next pull yanked him from his feet.

'Oops,' said Mo. 'I think it's still attached to his harness.'

'Never mind, keep going,' said Teejay.

Mr Toad thrashed as they dragged him to the bank. Then he scrambled from the water, one finger in the air. 'Victory! The Toad escapes again!' His eyes swivelled, and focused on Teejay. 'Toad Junior, did you see, did you see? A near-perfect test flight! And what a magnificent landing!'

Ratty blinked. 'That was magnificent?'

But Mr Toad wasn't listening. He unclipped his harness and raced around, gathering up bits of his paraglider. He stuffed them into a rucksack. 'All present and correct. Undamaged and airworthy!' he declared. He clapped both hands to his head. 'But my goodness, my precious pixies!'

'Your what?' said Ratty.

Mr Toad stared around frantically. 'My helmetty do-dah, where is it? It's of the utmost importance that I find it!'

Chapter 3
Clever Pixies

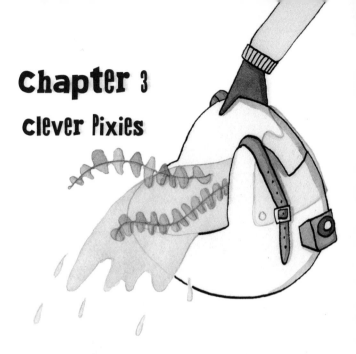

Everyone began searching around the pond.

'Hello, I just found this,' said a voice. Lennie walked up, holding a crash helmet. It had a camera strapped to the front. 'Does it belong to anyone?'

'It certainly does!' Mr Toad snatched it from her grasp. 'And I'll thank you to keep your paws off my property, young weasel.'

Lennie's face fell. 'I thought I was being nice.'

'That's what you weasels always say,' said Mr Toad. 'And then you steal a fellow's home.'

23

'I never stole anyone's home,' said Lennie.

'Hah!' Mr Toad raised his chin. 'It's only a matter of time.'

'Mr T, that's really rude!' Teejay frowned at him.

Mr Toad blinked. 'I beg your pardon?'

'Lennie just came out to help,' said Ratty.

'Right,' said Mo, 'and she found your helmet.'

'So you should say "thank you", and not be horrible,' Teejay finished.

Mr Toad hesitated. 'Very well. Perhaps I was too hasty.' He bowed to Lennie. 'Young lady, I apologize. I am grateful for your assistance. Now,' he handed the helmet to Mo, 'what do you make of this?'

Teejay peered over Mo's shoulder at the camera. It had the words 'ToadPro' written on the front.

'Ooh, those are the best you can get,' said Mo. 'They're waterproof *and* shockproof!'

'They'd have to be,' said Ratty.

'Precisely!' Mr Toad beamed. 'And they have lots of clever pixies.'

'Um, megapixels?' said Mo.

'Yes, those. And I need all of them for my aeronautic enterprises—' Mr Toad blinked. 'I say, what do all these people want?'

Teejay turned to see what he was looking at.
'Oh,' she said.

Ms Badger and Mr Polecat were standing
on the field, hands on their hips. Behind them
the rest of Teejay's class was pointing and
whispering.

'This is the culprit, Headmistress,' said Mr
Polecat. 'He was flying over the fields.'

Ms Badger glared at Mr Toad. 'There had
better be a *phenomenally* good reason for this.'

Mr Toad cleared his throat. 'Dear
Ms Badger, the fault is mine.'

'Yes, I think that's obvious,' said Ms Badger.

'My involuntary descent upon your educational establishment compelled these fine young animals to effect a daring rescue,' continued Mr Toad. 'Had it not been for their timely intervention I should have surely perished in the turbid clutches of your lake.'

'What's he saying?' hissed Teejay.

'We saved him from the pond,' Lennie whispered.

'In short, I owe them my life!' cried Mr Toad, one hand to his forehead.

'Don't be ridiculous, it's only knee-deep,' said Ms Badger. 'Now when you've quite finished disrupting lessons it's time you left.'

'Very well,' said Mr Toad, 'but I'll need to see young Mole after school. I need him to low-down the clever pixies.'

'What's he talking about?' said Mr Polecat.

'I think he wants to download some videos,' said Mo.

'Ooh, can we go, Badge?' said Teejay.

'That's "Ms Badger" in school, Teejay,' said Ms Badger. 'And only if you make up for the lesson you've interrupted.' She turned to Mr Toad. 'And I want you off our property, please.' She gave him a stern look. 'On foot.'

Chapter 4
The Great Director

Teejay, Ratty, and Mo pulled their bikes up at Toad Hall. Mr Toad was already waiting at the door. 'Where have you been?' he demanded. 'I expected you ages ago.'

'We had to catch up on lessons,' said Mo.

Ratty nodded. 'Ms Badger kept us for ages.'

'And she said you're not to get us into any trouble,' said Teejay, 'or she'll ban me from seeing you.'

'Clearly Ms Badger has no appreciation of the urgency of this situation.' Mr Toad ushered them through the door. 'Come along, quickly now.'

He ran off down Toad Hall's corridors. Teejay glanced at Ratty and Mo and they scampered after him. Mr Toad dashed to his study and leapt into a swivel chair. In front of him was a huge computer.

'What I'm about to reveal is a travesty of monumental proportions,' Mr Toad declared. 'We must direct all of our skill and cunning to its defeat.'

'Gosh,' said Teejay.

Mr Toad tapped at the keyboard. 'Here. Just look what it says on that infernal webby thing!'

'The internet?' said Mo.

'Whatever.' Mr Toad gestured at the screen. 'See what these blighters have written about Toad Hall.'

On the screen was a website. It read:

It's a wreck! The Willows Gossip Guide to Grand Houses in PIECES! You won't believe the state of these 'stately' homes! #1ToadHall

Below was an old photograph taken from high above Toad Hall. It showed a broken roof, and overgrown gardens tangled around a winding river. Beyond that were fields, leading to the dark mass of the Wild Wood. An arrow pointed at the house, with a label that said: *Toad-ally ruined!*

'Ruined?' cried Mr Toad. 'Can anyone see anything ruined around here? I rather think not!'

'It's just an out-of-date photo, Mr T,' said Teejay.

'And Toad Hall *was* a ruin before you fixed it,' Mo added.

'But it's not now! These interwebby scoundrels are peddling deceit.' Mr Toad glowered at the computer. 'My home is a thing of beauty and this morning's video will prove it!'

'Hang on,' said Ratty, 'you mean we stayed after school because you wanted a selfie with your house?'

'A small price for the honour of Toad Hall!' cried Mr Toad. He picked up the ToadPro and waved it at Mo. 'Now make this deliver my pixies!'

Mo sighed. He took the camera, pressed some buttons, then clicked the computer. 'OK, it's playing,' he said.

Mr Toad's screen went blotchy green, except for a blurry red square at the top.

'Is that meant to be Toad Hall's roof?' said Ratty, peering at it.

'Indeed! And the lawns below,' cried Mr Toad. 'It's rather artistic, isn't it?'

The video jerked, showing a slanted line of sky above some woodland. Teejay had to tilt her head to see it.

'Ah, the Wild Wood in its terrible beauty,' said Mr Toad. 'A triumph of the cinematographic medium.'

'A triumph of what?' whispered Teejay. Mo shrugged.

The video went blurry and focused on a high view of the school. The camera swooped over the roof. It turned and swooped again. Then it started spinning around.

'Urgh, I feel sick,' said Ratty.

The screen filled with Mr Toad's face, yelling in terror. And then it went black.

'Magnificent!' murmured Mr Toad. He stood tall and sang:

Toady! Toady! Flying right
Above Toad Hall just like a kite,
It takes his skilful hand and eye
To frame its repaired symmetry!

'There.' He sat back, looking pleased. 'And I think my video proves Toad Hall's a masterpiece!'

'No, it proves you can't use a camera,' said Ratty.

'Humph,' said Mr Toad.

'Sorry Mr T,' said Teejay, 'but it's a bit too blurry.'

'Oh, drat.' Mr Toad sagged. Then he brightened.

'But that simply means I must fly again! And with a little technical assistance my next film shall undoubtedly be a wonder!' Mr Toad grinned. 'What do you say, young Mole? Will you help me to master the pixies?'

Mo, though, was frowning at the screen. He rewound the video until it showed the Wild Wood. 'They're definitely not there,' he muttered. He switched to the picture of Toad Hall's ruins. 'They're here, but they're not there.'

'What are you talking about, Mo?' said Teejay.

'The trees!' Mo turned to her, eyes wide. 'They're all gone! Where have all the Wild Wood's trees gone?'

Chapter 5
Childish Squabbles

Mo zoomed in on an image. It showed Toad Hall's abandoned grounds, with Wild Wood stretching away, thick and dark.

'It looks like it always did,' said Mr Toad.

'Because that's the old photograph,' said Mo. 'Now look at this.'

He switched to a shot from Mr Toad's video.

Teejay gasped. 'Oh no!'

It was a blurry shot of the same patch of woods. But the image showed a giant clearing, with felled trunks scattered across the ground.

'Whoa,' said Ratty, 'who took all the trees?'

Mr Toad waved a hand. 'Bother the trees, what about my next flight?'

Teejay peered at the computer. 'What's that thing in the middle?'

Mo zoomed in on a yellow object. They peered at it.

'That,' said Ratty, 'looks like a very big digger.'

'Oh, they're cutting down the Wild Wood!' Mo squeaked. 'But who'd do that?'

'I bet it's the weasels,' said Teejay. 'Come on, Mr T, let's go and give them a talking-to!'

'What, and abandon my filming?'

'But if they keep going there won't be any woods left,' said Mo.

'I don't see the harm,' said Mr Toad. 'The Wild Wood is a ghastly place.'

'You said it had "terrible beauty",' said Ratty.

'Exactly: it's terrible,' said Mr Toad. 'It's chock-full of stoats for a start. If they want to cut it down, I say good luck to 'em.'

'You mean you don't care?' said Teejay.

'My dear Toad Junior, I have duties! I must devise a new flight plan and relaunch my paraglider. It's for the reputation of Toad Hall,' Mr Toad wagged a finger at her, 'and if you were any sort of Toad you'd be helping me, not starting childish squabbles with the weasels.'

Ratty stared at him. 'You *always* squabble with the weasels.'

'For noble causes, not over a bunch of silly trees!' cried Mr Toad.

'Trees aren't silly,' said Teejay, 'they're important! Everyone knows that.'

'Don't contradict your elders,' huffed Mr Toad. 'I say trees are silly, and so are you!'

'Ooh!' Teejay scowled at him. 'Ratty, Mo, I think we should go. Mr Toad is being a rotter. He's being a ne'er-do-well and a flibbertigibbet.' She marched to the door. 'And his flying wasn't very good!'

Mr Toad gasped. 'An insult! An affront! If that's how you feel then perhaps you *should* go to the weasels.'

'Don't worry, we're off!' Teejay cried. 'We'll do a proper protest and everything.'

'Hang on,' said Mo, 'I'm still busy with Mr Toad's video.'

'Aha! Here you see a fine and intelligent young animal,' declared Mr Toad. 'He's a Mole with his priorities straight!'

The printer on the desk whirred. Mo ran to it and took a stack of printouts.

'And what have you there, young Mole?' asked Mr Toad. 'Pictures of Toad Hall, perhaps? A new flight plan so I may capture the old place at its most glorious?'

'What?' Mo blinked. 'Oh. No, sorry. I just thought if we're going to protest then we should take some pictures of Wild Wood.'

'*Et tu*, Mole!' cried Mr Toad. He turned his back, chin in the air. 'Begone the lot of you. And don't come back until you've seen reason!'

'Fine,' said Teejay. 'We'll sort the weasels without you.'

'As usual,' Ratty added.

Mo packed up his pictures, and they walked from Toad Hall.

Chapter 6
Squashed Protest

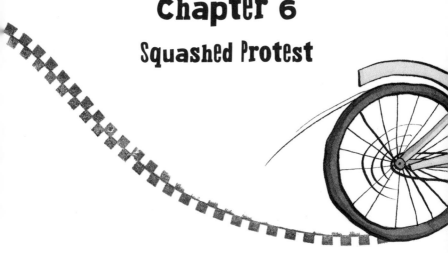

'**W**e'll show Mr Toad!' Teejay glared at the path as she cycled. 'And the weasels too, just see if we don't.'

'OK,' Mo panted, 'but can we do it slower? I'm really tired.'

'Don't be a moaning mole. Anyway, we're nearly there,' said Teejay. 'Look!'

Ahead was a pair of tall gates. Teejay skidded to a stop right beside them. Overhead was a sign that said:

welcome to wildwood Industrious:
Our ferrets will fell it!

Don't chop it or we'll get Ratty!
Paws off the wood!
Hey, weasels, leaf those trees Alone!

'Right, let's do our protest,' said Teejay. She hesitated. 'How do we protest?'

'We stand here and shout at people,' said Ratty.

'I don't like shouting,' said Mo. 'So I'll hold a sign. Look, I printed some.'

He showed them three sheets of paper. They said:

Paws Off the wood!

Hey, weasels, Leaf Those Trees Alone!

Don't chop it or we'll get Ratty!

'Mo, that's brilliant,' said Teejay. 'This is going to be the best protest ever!'

'Quick, there's a car coming,' said Ratty. 'Hand out the paper.'

A large, black car rolled out of Wildwood Industrious's gates. Teejay and Ratty shouted and Mo waved his sign. The car stopped next to them and a window slid down. The Chief Weasel glared out. Beside him sat a tall, grey weasel with a briefcase.

'Mr Ripton,' said the Chief Weasel, 'there appear to be children loose on our property. Should we call pest control? **Hurk hurk.**'

'We're not pests, we're protesting,' Mo squeaked.

'Because you're chopping down Wild Wood,' said Teejay.

'**Hurk hurk,**' laughed the Chief Weasel. 'This tiny toad says we're cutting down trees.

But the Wild Wood is protected, so that would
be illegal. Have you seen anything illegal going
on, Mr Ripton?'

The grey weasel frowned and shook his
head.

'There you have it,' said the Chief Weasel.
'Mr Ripton says there's nothing illegal. So it's
time for you to go home.'

Teejay heard a rumbling noise from further

down the road. Two trucks loaded with trunks roared up and disappeared through the gates.

'Hey, where did those trunks come from?' said Teejay.

Ratty held up one of Mo's pictures. 'And why's there a big digger in this clearing?'

The Chief Weasel hesitated. Mr Ripton whispered in his ear. 'Oh very good, Mr Ripton.' The Chief Weasel smiled nastily. 'Mr Ripton says that those trees were rotten. They all blew down in the last storm. So terribly sad. And of course we had to clear them away for safety reasons.' The smile slipped from the Chief Weasel's face. 'Now unless you have any *real* evidence, I advise you to go away.'

His car began to drive off. Then it stopped and pulled back. 'Oh, and I hope you're not thinking of going into the Wild Wood,' said the Chief Weasel. 'It's still rather unsafe. Lots of falling trees, that sort of thing. Small animals like you might get squished.' He smirked at Teejay. 'We wouldn't want to have to clear *you* up, now would we? **Hurk hurk.'**

The window wound up and the car motored away. Teejay sat down on the grass. 'Huh. I bet Wild Wood's trees didn't *really* fall over.'

'But how can we prove it?' said Mo.

'What if we caught them chopping trees? With a video or something?' said Teejay.

'You mean go into Wild Wood?' Ratty gulped. 'No way. We'll be squished. And that's not a good thing.'

'Oh, oh!' Mo got to his feet, excitedly. 'We don't have to go into the woods. We could fly *over* them instead!'

Ratty stared at him. 'That's worse.'

'No, Mo's right!' said Teejay. 'I mean we do know someone with a camera and a paraglider, right?'

'But Mr Toad's still cross with us. And he doesn't care about trees,' said Ratty.

'He will care,' said Mo. 'I know exactly how to get him to help. Come on, just follow my lead!'

He climbed back on his bike and started pedalling for Toad Hall.

Teejay grinned at Ratty and grabbed her bike. 'I love it when Mo has a plan.'

'Just as long as it doesn't get me squished,' muttered Ratty.

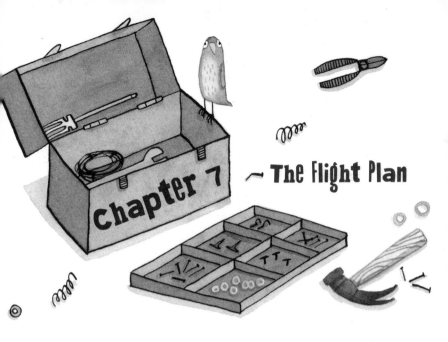

Mr Toad was out on Toad Hall's lawn with the paraglider in bits around him. He scowled at the children as they cycled up.

'If you've returned to babble about trees or insult my piloting prowess you should know that I'm very busy.' He held up his helmet and camera. 'My filming shall continue despite your mockery. Now, is there anything you'd like to say?'

'Good question,' whispered Teejay to Mo. 'What do we say?'

'We want to say sorry,' said Mo, loudly.

'Do we?' Ratty blinked.

'Yes, we do,' said Mo.

Teejay shrugged. 'OK. Then we're really sorry, Mr T.'

'Humph.' Mr Toad gave Ratty a suspicious look. 'Are *all* of you sorry?'

'If we have to be,' said Ratty. Teejay elbowed him. 'Ow! Yes, I'm sorry too.'

'Then the Toad is willing to forgive.' Mr Toad rubbed his hands together. 'And you're just in time to help me with the launch! I already have a magnificent flight plan prepared.' Mr Toad waved a piece of paper. It was covered in circles, splodges, and crossings out. 'What do you think?'

Ratty peered at it. 'I think you're heading for the school pond again.'

Mo pulled out a laptop. 'Mr Toad, I've been using my, um, technical wizardry. I have an idea for your flight plan.'

Mo tapped the laptop. The screen filled with a map, with bright lines on it.

Mr Toad stared. 'Are you quite certain? That appears to lead to the Wild Wood.'

'Of course,' said Mo. 'Your first video was out of focus because you were too close to Toad Hall. To get it right you need to be much further away.'

'And Toad Hall will look great from the woods,' said Teejay. 'It'll be really artistic.'

'You know, you might just have a point.' Mr Toad stroked his chin. 'I can picture it now: the savage wilds and the noble country estate, the woodland dwellings of the lowly stoats and the grand home of the gentleman Toad!'

'Exactly,' said Mo. 'So while you're over Wild Wood you should take lots of film of the trees.' He winked at Teejay. 'That way Toad Hall will look even better.'

'My dear young Mole, your plan is superb,' said Mr Toad. He frowned at the screen. 'But how can I be certain I'm following the correct path?'

'We'll guide you!' Ratty opened his bag and pulled out two walkie-talkies. He gave one to Mr Toad. 'I always have these with me.'

'Brilliant, Rat,' said Teejay. 'We'll be able to talk to Mr T from miles away.'

Mr Toad's eyes shone. He pressed the button on the handset. 'Hello!' he yelled into it. 'Can you hear me?'

'Yes.' Ratty rubbed his ear. 'Because I'm right beside you.'

'My apologies,' said Mr Toad. 'Now, quickly, help me set up.'

They got him into his flying harness, and spread the wing out on the lawn behind him.

'Excellent!' Mr Toad strapped on his flying helmet and camera. 'Now fetch my final piece of equipment.'

'This?' Mo grabbed a bag almost bigger than he was. 'Oof! It's heavy!'

'Down here it may be,' Mr Toad took it from him, 'but this device will transform me. No longer shall I drift like thistledown, but soar like the swiftest of falcons.'

Inside the bag was something that looked like a giant fan with straps.

'Oh!' squeaked Mo. 'It's a paraglider motor!'

'It certainly is!' Mr Toad put it on his back and held up his walkie-talkie. 'Toad Junior, I'm putting you in charge of communications.'

'Yes sir!' Teejay saluted.

'Excellent. Now clear the runway and get to the roof.' Mr Toad turned to face the Wild Wood. 'The hour is upon us when the Toad shall take flight!'

Chapter 8

A Textbook Take-off

Teejay, Ratty, and Mo dashed up Toad Hall's stairs, heading for the attic. Teejay pulled open the door and they ran out onto a flat roof, right at the top of the house.

Teejay leaned over the balcony. She pressed the button on her walkie-talkie. 'We're in position, Mr T!'

Teejay's handset crackled. *Tzzzk. 'Toad here. Good show. Stand by. Over.'* *Tzzzk.*

Teejay pressed the button. 'Right. Um, good show,' she said. 'Over.'

Tzzzk. 'Toad here. Preparations complete.

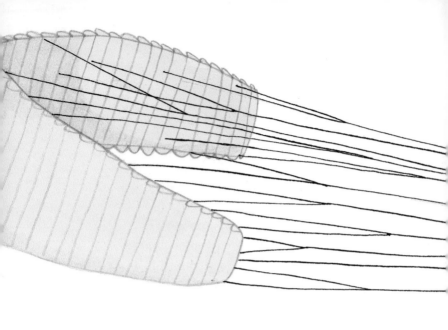

Commence countdown. Over.' *Tzzzk.*

Teejay grinned at Ratty and Mo. 'I always wanted to do this.' She pressed the button on the handset. 'Five!' she shouted. 'Four!'

Tzzzk. 'Ignition!' Tzzzk.

The paraglider's motor spluttered, then began to whir.

vRRRR-vRRRRR-vRRRRROOAAZZZZZZZZZZZZZZZZZZZZZZZZ

'Three,' cried Teejay.

'Two!' Ratty and Mo joined in. 'One!'

'Go, go, go!' yelled Teejay.

Tzzzk. 'Tally-ho!' Tzzzk.

Mr Toad ran forwards. Behind him the paraglider wing rose into the air. He sprinted faster.

Tzzzk. 'Take-off speed . . . optimal,' Mr Toad

panted. *Tzzzk.* *'Gently increasing throttle . . .'*
VRAAAAZZZZZZZZZZZZZZZ!

The paraglider lurched forwards, yanking
Mr Toad into the air. He hauled at the controls
and the paraglider turned. Then it dived at the
ground.

'Eek!' Mo covered his eyes.

Just in time the paraglider swept upwards,
carrying Mr Toad over the river. His feet
crashed through the treetops.

Tzzzk. *'Ouch.'* *Tzzzk.*

'He's up, he's up!' cried Teejay.

Mr Toad steered around in a wobbly circle.
The paraglider swerved and jerked.

'Great. Do you think he's going to stay up?'
said Ratty.

Tzzzk. *'Toad here. Have executed textbook
take-off. Awaiting instructions.'* *Tzzzk.*

Mo opened his laptop and showed Teejay
the flight plan.

'It says "proceed east to Wild Wood",' said
Teejay.

Tzzzk. 'Which way is east?' Tzzzk.

Mo leaned over Teejay's handset. 'Head for the big green thing full of trees and weasels.'

Tzzzk. 'Wilco. Roger that. Proceeding weaselward. Over.' Tzzzk.

vRRAAzzzzzzzzzzzzzzzzzzzzzzzzzzzzzzzzzzzzzzzzzzzzz

The paraglider buzzed away over the fields towards the Wild Wood.

'He's going really fast!' cried Teejay. 'He already looks small.'

Ratty pulled out a pair of binoculars. 'And he's almost flying straight. Maybe he's getting the hang of it.'

Tzzzk. 'Toad here. I say, there's a handle marked "Emergency Release". Any clue what it does? Over.' Tzzzk.

'Don't pull it!' Mo shouted into the walkie-talkie.

'I take it back,' said Ratty. 'He's going to crash.'

They watched Mr Toad's tiny paraglider heading to the distant woods.

'Don't worry, Rat,' said Teejay, 'what's the worst that could happen?'

Ratty gave her a look. 'Why do you always have to ask that?'

Chapter 9

~~Soar Like a Falcon~~ Tumble Like a Toad

The walkie-talkie crackled.

Tzzzk. 'Toad here. Have reached the Wild Wood. Lots of trees. Toad Hall looks jolly fine. Excellent film footage. Over.' Tzzk.

'That's great, Mr T,' said Teejay into the handset. 'Don't forget to film the woods.'

Tzzzk. 'Roger that. Good gracious! That's enormous!' Tzzzk.

'What?' said Teejay. 'What's enormous?'

Tzzzk. 'Huge bald patch. Trees missing and teeming with stoaty types.' Tzzzk.

'That must be the clearing,' said Mo.

'He's caught them cutting down trees!' said Ratty.

'Are you filming, Mr T?' said Teejay, anxiously.

Tzzzk. 'Indeed, I have pixies full of ferrets! Over.' Tzzzk.

'He's got them on video!' Mo said. 'We should get him back. The weasels won't be happy if they spot him.'

'Good point,' said Teejay. She pressed the button. 'Mr T, the flight plan says to come straight back to Toad Hall.'

Tzzzk. 'Incoming flak. Spotted by enemy. Weasels issuing rude instructions. Preparing to return fire. Over.' Tzzzk.

'No, no, bad idea. Is he coming back, Rat?' said Mo.

Ratty raised the binoculars. 'Yes, he's turning . . . oh, no, he's going around again. He's diving lower. And he's shouting something.'

Tzzzk. 'Haha! I am every weasel's nightmare. I'm a motor-equipped aeronautical

Toad! I'll give you the what-for, you tree-harming ninnies! Thhhhuuuurrrrp!' Tzzzk.

'Oh dear,' said Teejay, 'he's blowing raspberries.'

Tzzzk. 'Haha! I'm flying to foil your foul felling you scurrilous stoats, you wretched work weasels! Cut down the woods will you? Well thuuuurrrrp to you!' Tzzzk.

'But he said he didn't care about trees,' said Mo.

Teejay shrugged. 'I think he just likes shouting at weasels.'

Ratty's paws clenched on the binoculars. 'He's not looking where he's going. Tell him to pull up, he's too low!'

'Mr Toad,' said Teejay, urgently, 'Ratty says—'

Tzzzk. '*I'm Toad at my highest, I'm over your woods,*

And you cannot stop me, I'm up here for good,

I'll shout what I like and I have not a care,

For you're down on the ground and I'm high in the air!

Haha! Thuuurrrp!' Tzzzk.

Teejay tried again. 'Mr Toad, you have to go higher. You're going to hit the trees!'

Tzzzk. 'Nonsense, I'm perfectly in control. I'm—yikes!' Tzzzk.

Crashing and snapping noises, cursing and shouting came over the walkie-talkie. Then there was a loud *Tzzzk*, and the handset went quiet.

Teejay stared at Ratty and Mo. She pressed the button. 'Mr T, are you OK?'

Tzzzk. 'Mayday, Mayday, this is Toad requesting assistance. Had altercation with tree. Am unavoidably detained in an inverted position. Over.' Tzzzk.

'Oh no, he's hanging upside down!' cried Mo.

'Where are you?' said Teejay. 'Are you OK?'

Tzzzk. 'Can you hear me? I'm caught in a tree. Mayday, Mayday!' Tzzzk.

'We can hear you, Mr T,' said Teejay. 'Can't you hear us?'

Tzzzk. 'Oh please? Toad Junior? My good Rat and Mole? Anyone? Please don't tell me I'm stuck here alone.' Tzzzk.

'He can't hear us! We've got to help him!' said Teejay.

'But how?' said Ratty. 'He's in the Wild Wood.'

'Surrounded by weasels,' said Mo.

'Annoyed weasels,' Ratty added.

'Then we have to get him out.' Teejay frowned. 'We must know someone who can help.'

'Yes, we do: Ms Badger,' said Mo.

'Badge?' Teejay stared at him. 'Don't we know anyone else? I promised her I'd stay out of trouble.'

'How's that working out for you?' said Ratty.

Teejay put her head in her hands. 'Oh *no*. I'm never going to be allowed out again.'

Chapter 10
The wild wood

Ms Badger drove them down the road towards the trees. 'Here we are,' she said. 'This is the start of the Wild Wood. And if Mr Toad's in there we'd better find him quickly.'

Teejay gazed out of the car window. The woods looked dark and tangled.

'I still don't know who gave Mr Toad the idea of flying over here,' Ms Badger continued, 'and right now I don't care. But somebody, probably Teejay, is going to be in a lot of trouble later on. Understood?'

Teejay stared at the floor of the car. 'Yes, Badge.'

'Just so long as you know,' said Ms Badger.

The road ended at a pair of high, wooden gates, shut tight. Next to them a weasel in a yellow jacket and hard hat dozed in a chair. But before they reached him Ms Badger took a half-hidden track, and parked the car behind some bushes.

'We'll be out of sight here,' she said.

In front of the car, almost lost in the leaves, was a dark gap in the fence. It was just big enough to squeeze through.

'That's the old way into the woods,' Ms Badger said. 'Not even the weasels would dare block it off.' She turned to Teejay, Ratty,

snore snore

and Mo. 'Right, you lot, I'm going in to find Mr Toad. You will wait here.' She frowned at Teejay. 'I mean it, Teejay: in the car. And keep out of sight.'

'Can't we come too?' said Teejay.

'We could help you look,' said Ratty.

Ms Badger shook her head. 'The Wild Wood isn't as fearful as it was, but small animals can still find trouble.' She looked away at the trees. 'If you don't know the passwords and signs it's best you stay here.'

Teejay shivered. 'Will . . . will you be all right?'

Ms Badger smiled. 'I'm a Badger. This is where I spent my cubhood.' Her eyes narrowed. 'And believe me, nobody in there will mess with me.' She got out of the car. 'I'll be back soon. Stay put.'

Teejay watched her walk away into the Wild Wood. Ms Badger slipped between the trees and was lost from view.

'Is it me,' said Mo, 'or was that a bit scary?'

'That was a *lot* scary,' said Ratty.

'Huh.' Teejay folded her arms. 'I still think we could have gone too.'

'Oh well,' said Mo. 'Anyone fancy a game of I-spy?'

Teejay sighed. 'Not really.'

'Come on,' said Mo, 'I'll start . . . I spy with my little eye something beginning with "W".'

'Worm?' said Ratty.

'No.'

'Woods?'

'No,' said Mo. 'Too easy.'

'Weasel!' Teejay cried.

'No,' Mo scoffed, 'if I'd seen a weasel I'd—
ouf!'

Teejay grabbed him and dragged him to
the floor of the car. 'No, there is a weasel,' she
hissed. 'Look!'

They peeked out of the window. At the gap
in the fence a pointed face was peering left
and right. Then a weasel dashed out, heading
towards the main gate.

'Wesley!' yelled the weasel. 'Wesley, we've
caught old Toady!'

'It's about Mr Toad.' Teejay opened the car door. 'I need to hear what they're saying.'

She slipped from the car and hid behind a tree, just out of sight.

The weasel at the gates rubbed his eyes. 'What you talking about, Wilbur?'

'It's Toady!' said Wilbur. 'He's in the clearing, hanging off a tree.'

'Why's he doing that?' said Wesley.

'I don't think it's on purpose, Wes,' said Wilbur. 'Anyhow, phone the

Executive, will you? He'll be proper chuffed.
I reckon old Toady would give anything to get
down.'

Wesley grinned. 'Like his house, you mean?'

'Exactly!' Wilbur turned to go.

'Where are you off to?'

'I'm going to make sure Toady stays put,' Wilbur grinned. 'At least until the Chief gets here.'

He did not glance at Ms Badger's car, but headed back to the woods. He slipped through the fence, and disappeared into the trees.

Chapter 11

whistles and weasels

Teejay sprinted back to the car. 'That weasel knows where Mr Toad is!' She pulled the door open. 'We've got to follow him!'

Ratty stared at her. 'No way! That's the Wild Wood.'

'And Ms Badger said we shouldn't,' said Mo.

'But the Chief Weasel's coming. And Mr T's hanging from a tree,' said Teejay. 'They'll make him give them Toad Hall, or all his money or something. Come on!'

Mo put his head in his paws. 'This is going to be horrible.'

'Yes, it really is,' said Ratty.

'So you'll do it?' said Teejay. She grinned at them. 'Good work! Let's go!'

They dashed for the gap in the fence, then stepped cautiously into the Wild Wood. They walked quietly, creeping from tree to tree. Ahead they saw flashes of the weasel's yellow jacket through the branches. The path he followed was faint and narrow. It split, then split again and again.

'I don't like this,' Mo whimpered. 'Even if we find Mr Toad we'll never get back.'

'Don't worry,' said Teejay. 'The woods can't be that big.'

But long minutes passed and the Wild Wood closed around them. It was chill and dark. The birds grew quiet in the trees above. And soon the only sounds were the rustle of their footsteps, and their breathing.

'I like it here,' said Ratty. 'It's nice.'

'Really?' said Teejay.

'No,' Ratty shuddered. 'Not really.'

A low whistle echoed off the trees.

'What was that?' Mo squeaked.

Another whistle, then another answered. And then strange, high-pitched laughter echoed from the trees. Something crashed in the bushes ahead.

Ratty grabbed Teejay's shoulder. 'Quick,' he hissed. 'Hide!'

They scuttled behind a fallen tree and crouched there, shivering. The crashing sounds, laughs, and whistles got louder.

'Alright, Wilbur,' called a voice. 'Where're you off to?'

Teejay spied three weasels through the branches. They wore bright jackets and hard hats. And they carried chainsaws and axes.

'Back to the Deep Wood clearing,' said Wilbur. 'Is Old Toady still in his tree?'

Teejay heard chuckles. 'Yep, and he's not too happy about it,' said one weasel. 'Called me a "bounder".'

'He says I'm a "rapscallion",' said another. 'If

I was the Chief I'd leave him there.'

'Nah,' said the first weasel, 'you know what the Chief's like. He'll do anything for a posh house. Anyway, come on, lads, it's home time.'

Teejay waited until the weasels were gone. She got up from behind the log.

'Those weasels had axes,' she said. 'Do you know what that means?'

'Yes, they're really dangerous,' said Ratty.

'It means they've been chopping down trees,' said Mo.

'Right! And Mr Toad's in the clearing,' grinned Teejay. 'So our weasel's on the right track.'

Ratty glanced around. 'Um, where *is* our weasel?'

Teejay stared at the woods. Nothing moved. Everything was still, and quiet.

'Oh no, he's vanished!' cried Mo. 'We're doomed!'

'Don't panic, Mo,' said Teejay. 'Those weasels came from the clearing, so we just

have to go where they came from.'

She set off. Ratty and Mo ran after her.

'Is this a good idea?' said Mo.

'Of course not,' said Ratty, 'we're heading towards a load of weasels with axes.'

'Oh, stop complaining,' said Teejay. 'It's easy: we keep going, rescue Mr Toad, and leave. There's no way we'll get lost.'

Chapter 12

'KEEP OUT!'

Teejay scowled at the trees.

'We're lost, aren't we?' said Ratty.

'*We're* in the right place,' said Teejay. 'It's the wood that's all wrong.'

They had been walking for ages. The path had disappeared and there was no sign of any clearing.

'We're lost, we're lost!' Mo slumped against a tree. 'We're in the Wild Wood and we're lost.'

'And the weasels have axes,' said Ratty. 'Don't forget that.'

A whistle pierced the air. It was high and shrill.

Mo leapt up. 'Eek, axe-weasels!'

'Quick,' said Teejay, 'get off the path!'

She and Ratty dragged Mo into a bush.

'Ow, brambles!' said Mo.

'Shh, they'll hear us. Get down.' Teejay crouched, trying to keep small.

Footsteps came closer. Another whistle rang out. Then more footsteps . . . that stopped. Teejay shivered. The weasel must be right by

their hiding place.

'Oh hello!' said a voice. 'I thought I heard something rustling. Isn't it a bit spiky in there?'

Teejay blinked up through the brambles. Staring down at them was Lennie, still wearing her school rucksack. In one paw was a bunch of flowers.

'What are you doing here?' Teejay scrambled to her feet. 'We thought you were a weasel!'

Lennie giggled. 'I *am* a weasel. I went for a walk. It's so lovely in Wild Wood.'

'Lovely?' Ratty stared. 'Is that a new word for "horrible"?'

'It's scary,' sniffed Mo. 'We're lost and people keep whistling at us.'

'Oh, you have to whistle, it's one of the rules,' said Lennie. 'But I never thought it could be frightening.'

'Lennie, can you help us,' cried Teejay. 'Mr Toad's stuck up a tree!'

'That's terrible!' said Lennie. 'Where is he?'

'In the clearing,' said Ratty.

'In the Deep Wood,' added Mo. 'The axe-weasels said so.'

Lennie looked puzzled. 'There isn't a clearing in the Deep Wood. But anyway, I can take you there!'

She set off, moving so quickly that the others had to jog to keep up. The path twisted and forked, but Lennie did not hesitate. Sometimes she stopped and whistled, then moved on. The woods were still scary, Teejay thought, but she felt better with Lennie guiding them.

'It's not far now,' said Lennie. 'Just through the next—oh!'

Ahead of them a gravel road ran off through the woods in both directions. Lennie stared at it. 'This used to be the Whistling Way. It was the main path . . . and now it's a road.'

Beside Teejay was a sign that said:

KEEP OUT! WORKERS REPORT
TO THE FORE-FERRET.
THE DEEP WOOD IS CLOSED BY
ORDER OF THE EXECUTIVE.

'This must be where they're chopping trees,' said Ratty.

'Chopping trees?' scoffed Lennie. 'Don't be silly. People live here.' A low rumble echoed through the Wild Wood. 'Oh, there's a lorry coming. Maybe they can tell us what's happening.'

Lennie stepped onto the track. But Teejay and Ratty bundled her back into the trees. The truck rumbled past. Inside weasels were laughing and chatting, and the back was piled high with trunks. It disappeared off down the road.

'Sorry, Lennie,' said Teejay, 'but we don't want to be seen.'

Lennie stared after the truck. 'Those were weasels! And tree trunks!' Her paws clenched. 'You're right, there is something going on.' She turned to Teejay. 'How do we find out what it is?'

Chapter 13
weasonably
unwecognizable

They dashed alongside the Whistling Way, keeping off the path. They passed parties of weasels heading off from work. Again and again the children had to dive for cover.

Mo picked burrs off his fur. 'Oh, I hate this.'

'It *would* be easier to walk down the track,' said Lennie.

'We need to stay hidden,' said Teejay. 'Then we can see what's happening without being spotted.'

'Like secret spies, you mean?' said Lennie. She paused. 'Hey, what if I could find you weasel disguises? Look over there!'

Half-hidden in trees was a wooden shack. Through the window Teejay glimpsed rows of jackets and helmets hanging up.

'That's where they keep their work clothes,' said Mo.

Teejay smiled. 'Lennie, you're a genius.'

Lennie sneaked up to the shack and peeked through the window. 'Nobody home. Wait

here.' She disappeared around the corner. Teejay heard a door creak, and moments later Lennie returned, paws full of overalls, safety jackets, helmets, and goggles.

'This is brilliant!' Teejay put on work trousers and a jacket. 'Do I look like a weasel yet?'

'No, your hands are green. You need gloves,' said Ratty. He climbed into overalls. 'And my tail's the wrong shape.'

Teejay put on a helmet. 'Just tuck it into your clothes, no one will know.'

'What about my nose?' said Mo.

Lennie handed him a dust mask and safety goggles. 'Put these on,' she said. 'You'll look great!'

'No, he'll look stupid,' said Ratty.

Soon Teejay, Ratty, and Mo were in helmets, dust masks, and goggles. Teejay grinned at her friends. 'They'll never spot us now.'

'And if they do they'll be too busy laughing to chase us,' Ratty muttered.

'Come on, let's test the costumes!' Teejay stepped onto the Whistling Way and they walked towards the clearing. By the roadside a last group of stoats was packing up their tools.

'What do we do, what do we do?' Mo fretted.

'Just nod and smile,' said Lennie. 'And don't forget to whistle.'

Teejay held her breath as they got closer. A stoat nodded at her, then went back to his packing.

'Phew, it worked,' said Ratty when they were past. 'And look, there's the clearing!'

A short distance away lorries were parked in front of a huge, empty circle. It was surrounded by distant trees, and logs and sawdust covered the ground. Here and there lay empty diggers.

Lennie's bottom lip quivered. 'Why would anyone do this?' She turned to Teejay. 'It used to be so beautiful.'

Teejay gave her a hug. 'Don't worry, we'll find Mr Toad and make them put it back. I promise.'

But before she could move she heard a weasel's voice behind her.

'Hey, you! What do you reckon you're doing, then?'

Chapter 14
Hanging Around

Teejay spun to see a weasel walking towards them.

'Who are you lot? Did the Chief send you?' said the weasel.

'Yes, that's right,' said Teejay. 'I'm Wilbur the weasel.'

The weasel stopped dead. 'Hang on, *I'm* Wilbur.'

'Oh,' said Teejay, 'then I meant "William".'

Wilbur frowned, but before he could speak, Lennie stepped forward.

'Hello, Wilbur,' she said. 'Lovely day isn't it?'

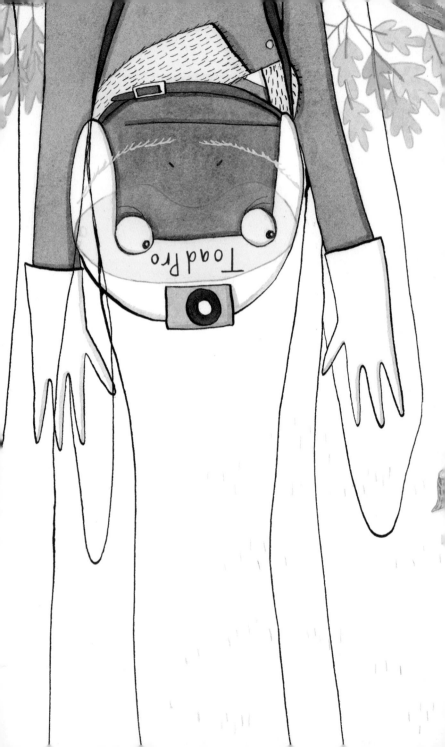

'Oh, Miss Lenora! I didn't see you.' Wilbur glanced around, and lowered his voice. 'Um, it's not my place, miss, but does the Executive know you're here? The clearing's really only for work-weasels. Bit dangerous with all the trees.'

'It's OK,' said Lennie, 'he sent, um, William along to take care of me. We're looking for Mr Toad.'

'Oh, that's different,' said Wilbur, looking relieved. 'If it's OK with the Chief, it's fine with me. Old Toady's hanging around over there.'

At the far side of the clearing was an immense tree. Mr Toad was dangling upside down from the very highest branch. A gust of wind made him swing.

'Wow. He's a *long* way up,' Ratty hissed.

'I know, right!' Wilbur grinned. 'This time we've got him right where we want him.' He paused. 'Um, Miss Lenora, you wouldn't mind keeping an eye on him for a bit? Just I'm desperate for a cup of tea.'

'Don't worry, Wilbur,' said Lennie, 'we'll look after Mr Toad.'

'Thanks, miss. And don't tell your Dad, eh? I wouldn't want the Chief thinking I wasn't doing my job.'

Wilbur wandered away. Teejay, Ratty, and Mo stared at Lennie.

'What?' said Lennie.

'The Chief Weasel's your *dad*?' said Ratty.

'Of course,' said Lennie.

'But—but—' Mo began.

'You there!' Mr Toad's voice yelled down from the tree. 'Don't think I can't see you skulking in the shadows!'

'Is he talking to us?' said Teejay.

'Come for a stoat-gloat have you?' cried Mr Toad. 'Think it's funny, leaving old Toady dangling in this dingy dell? Nothing to say, you dollop of dismal dunderheads?'

'He's not very pleased to see us, is he?' said Ratty.

'He thinks we're weasels,' said Mo. 'We're disguised, remember?'

'That's no reason to be rude.' Lennie raised her voice. 'Mr Toad, we'll get you down but only if you ask nicely!'

Mr Toad peered at her. 'I say, aren't you that fine young lady who gave me back my flying helmet?'

'That's right,' called Lennie. 'And the others

aren't really weasels, they're—'

'At last!' cried Mr Toad. 'A sensible and compassionate young weasel. Oh, please take pity on an unfortunate Toad and free me from this arboreal abomination!'

'Does he always talk like that?' Lennie whispered.

'You get used to it,' said Teejay. She raised her voice. 'Hang on, we're on our way!'

'Oh, thank you, thank you, noble stoat,' said Mr Toad. 'But please hurry!'

'Right, troops,' said Teejay to the others, 'this is mission Toad rescue. We'll keep disguised and work quickly and be back at the car before Badge knows we're gone. It's foolproof.'

'Unless someone catches us or Ms Badger finds out,' said Ratty.

'Exactly,' Teejay grinned. 'Let's do it!'

And they ran towards the tree.

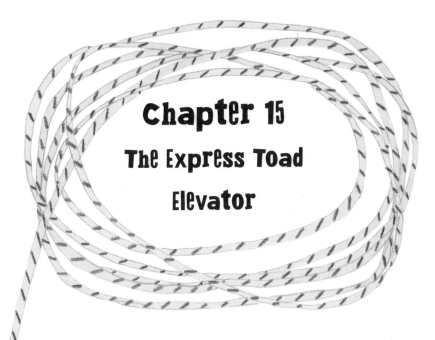

Chapter 15
The Express Toad Elevator

Teejay stared up the trunk. Only the top half of Mr Toad could be seen hanging upside down through the highest branches. 'Any ideas?' she said.

'We could lower him on a rope,' said Mo. 'Except we don't have one.'

'That's what you think.' Ratty took off his rucksack and pulled out a coil of rope. 'Ta-da!'

'Brilliant, Rat!' cried Teejay. 'We just climb up there and tie it to him.' She squinted at Mr Toad, tiny above her. She gulped. 'Any volunteers?'

'I'm not going up there!' said Mo.

'Me neither,' said Ratty. 'I'll stay and hold the rope.'

'I'll do it,' said Lennie. 'Weasels are good at climbing.' She slung the rope over her shoulder, then scampered up onto the first branch. Then she shot up the tree like a squirrel.

'Wow,' said Ratty, 'she's amazing.'

'Huh. I could have gone if I wanted to,' said Teejay.

Soon Lennie was hidden among the leaves and high

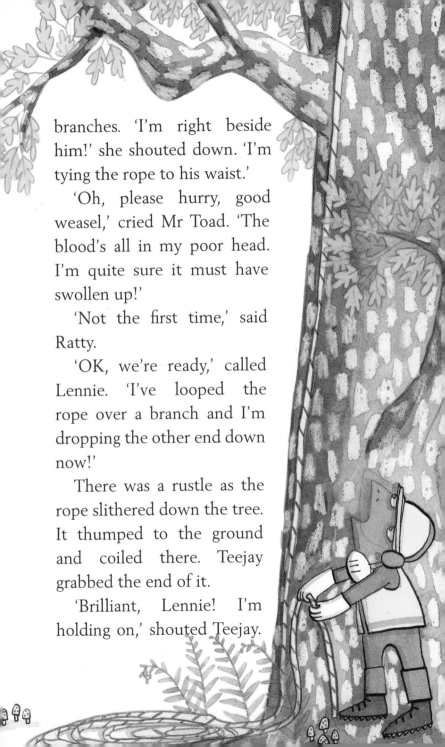

branches. 'I'm right beside him!' she shouted down. 'I'm tying the rope to his waist.'

'Oh, please hurry, good weasel,' cried Mr Toad. 'The blood's all in my poor head. I'm quite sure it must have swollen up!'

'Not the first time,' said Ratty.

'OK, we're ready,' called Lennie. 'I've looped the rope over a branch and I'm dropping the other end down now!'

There was a rustle as the rope slithered down the tree. It thumped to the ground and coiled there. Teejay grabbed the end of it.

'Brilliant, Lennie! I'm holding on,' shouted Teejay.

'Undo his harness!'

'Right!' said Lennie.

'No, wait, the rope's too short,' said Mo.

'What do you mean? I've got hold of it, haven't I?' said Teejay.

'Yes, but— ' Mo began.

Before he could finish, Teejay heard a crunch of gravel. A long, black car rolled down the track. It stopped at the edge of the clearing and two figures got out. They started walking towards the tree.

'Argh, it's the Chief Weasel!' hissed Ratty. 'Now what do we do?'

'Act like stoats,' said Teejay.

'How?' said Mo.

'I don't know. Look pointy.'

The Chief Weasel did not even glance at them. Instead he walked to the tree and peered up through the branches.

'**Hurk hurk,**' he chuckled. 'Mr Ripton, I thought I knew all the local wildlife. But look, I've discovered a new tree frog.'

Mr Ripton smiled.

'Are you ready?' shouted Lennie from above. 'I'm undoing the final buckle!'

'Is there someone else up there?' The Chief Weasel glared up the tree. 'Who gave you permission to lower the Toad? Stop what you're doing!'

Click!

The harness came undone. The rope on the ground uncoiled with a hiss. It flew up into the tree.

And Mr Toad plummeted, yelling, towards them.

Teejay held tight as the coil ran out.

The rope snapped taut.

And then it yanked her into the air, hurtling up into the tree.

Chapter 16
Your Dangling Days are Done

Limbs and branches, twigs and leaves, whipped past Teejay as she flew.

'Stop, stop, stop!' she cried. The end of a branch raced towards her. She swerved, just in time. It caught in her overalls and she jerked to a stop.

Rrriiiipp!

Her trousers began to tear. Above her the rope stretched into the canopy. And at the foot of the tree Mr Toad bounced, mere inches above the Chief Weasel's head.

'This . . . this isn't good,' Teejay gasped.

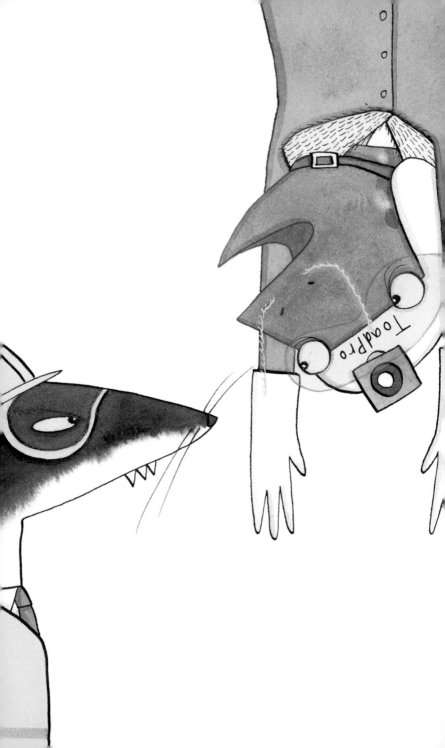

Her gloves began to slip. 'Lennie, help, I can't hold on!'

'Don't worry, I'm coming!' Lennie scrambled down towards her.

'Hurry!' Teejay glanced down and wished she hadn't. Ratty and Mo were tiny below her.

The Chief Weasel was grinning at Mr Toad. 'Oh look, Mr Ripton, it wasn't a tree frog at all. It was a lesser-spotted bungy-jumping interference. Nice of him to, ah, drop in. **Hurk hurk.**'

Mr Toad's eyes snapped open. They focused on the Chief Weasel.

'You!' cried Mr Toad. 'You dastardly tree-clearing menace! Be warned that I have captured your villainous exploits on film. I insist that you release me immediately.'

'You, Mr Toad, are in no position to insist on anything.' The Chief Weasel walked right under him. He gazed up at Mr Toad, nose to nose. 'In fact, I believe that Mr Ripton and I have some insisting of our own to do. For example, we insist that you give us Toad Hall. **Hurk hurk.'** The Chief Weasel lit a cigar and blew the smoke in Mr Toad's face. 'Doesn't that sound good, Mr Toad? We let you down and Wildwood Industrious gets a lovely new place to build weasel homes.'

Mr Ripton undid his briefcase and pulled out a sheet of paper.

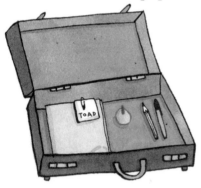

'All you have to do is sign, Mr Toad,' said the Chief Weasel. 'And then your dangling days are done.'

Mr Toad's eyes widened. 'Never! I shall go to the police with my film.'

The Chief Weasel picked Mr Toad's helmet up from the ground. 'You mean *this* film? Taken illegally on Wildwood Industrious's property. Tut tut. Perhaps we should hang onto that, Mr Ripton?'

Mr Ripton nodded. The Chief Weasel turned to go. 'Enjoy your stay, Mr Toad. We'll be back when you're ready to talk. Maybe a day or two.'

Teejay heard a rustle above her, and Lennie clambered onto the branch. She grabbed the back of Teejay's trousers.

'I've got you,' she said. 'Let go of the rope!'

'Are you sure?' said Teejay.

'Promise!'

Teejay let go. The rope whisked through her gloves and Lennie pulled her to safety.

'Phew,' said Teejay. 'Thanks, Lennie. Now let's get down.'

From below them came a loud *thump!*

Mr Toad had fallen right on top of the Chief Weasel.

'Get off me you overbearing amphibian!'

Mr Toad clambered to his feet. He grabbed the helmet from the Chief Weasel's paws.

'Hah!' he cried. 'My pixies.'

But the Chief Weasel leapt up and snatched it back. 'The helmet is ours,' he snarled. He poked Mr Toad in his chest. 'I'll do what I like in my own woods. Who cares about some nasty damp trees, when Wildwood Industrious has weasels to pay?'

'I do.' Lennie dropped from the tree and ran to the Chief Weasel's side. 'Daddy, did you really cut down the woods? Please say you didn't.'

The Chief Weasel's jaw fell open. He stared at his daughter. 'Ah,' he said. 'Um.' He looked at Mr Ripton, who started fiddling with his briefcase. 'Well, I suppose I did, yes. But don't worry, love, all our weasels will get new homes.'

'And what about the other animals? Where will they live?' Lennie gestured at the clearing. 'They won't get new homes.' A tear trickled down her cheek. 'This used to be my favourite place. And you've made it horrible.'

Lennie sat on the ground and started to cry. The Chief Weasel looked helplessly down at his daughter. Nobody spoke.

Then, with a rustle, Ms Badger stepped from the trees across the clearing. She scowled at the group and set off, striding towards them.

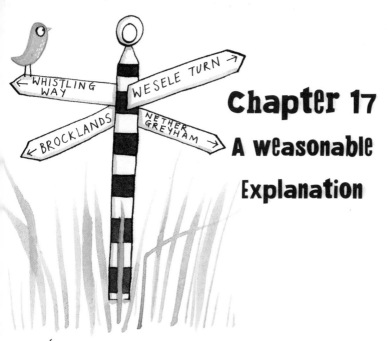

Chapter 17
A weasonable
Explanation

'**There** you are, Mr Toad,' called Ms Badger. 'I've been searching all over the Wild Wood for you.'

'She looks angry,' said Mo.

'We need to go,' Ratty hissed to Teejay. 'Now.'

'Yes we do,' Teejay whispered. 'Let's move!'

They started sidling away around the edge of the clearing.

'You weasels stay right where you are,' growled Ms Badger. Teejay froze as she marched past. She went up to the Chief Weasel

and folded her arms. 'What on earth has been happening here? Don't you know these woods are protected!'

'That's right, Daddy!' Lennie wiped her nose on her paw. 'They're protected. Why did you do this?'

The Chief Weasel looked desperately from Ms Badger to Lennie. He glanced at Mr Ripton, who was now examining a leaf.

'I think I can explain,' said Mr Toad. He stepped forwards and clasped his hands in front of him. 'But first, my dear Ms Badger, I should thank you for coming to my assistance. I've been a very silly Toad indeed.'

'As usual,' said Ms Badger. 'Now explain.'

'Nothing simpler,' said Mr Toad. 'The Chief Weasel was just telling me how Wildwood Industrious has been clearing away some dangerous trees. Weren't you, Chief Weasel?'

The Chief Weasel and Mr Ripton's jaws were open. They nodded, silently.

'What's Mr T doing?' hissed Teejay.

138

Mo smiled. 'I think he's making it right.'

'And now the trees are all safe,' continued Mr Toad, 'he tells me he's going to replant the woods. Every last tree. Isn't that right, Chief Weasel?'

Lennie dried her tears. She jumped up and clutched the Chief Weasel's hand. 'Oh Daddy, is that true? Please tell me it is.'

'Yes,' said the Chief Weasel in a strangled voice. 'Yes, darling, of course it is. I'd never cut down your favourite woods.'

Lennie hugged him. 'Oh, I knew you wouldn't do anything bad!'

The Chief Weasel patted her head, then gently pulled away. He sidled over to Mr Toad. 'All right, Toady,' he snarled. 'I owe you this one. But you've just cost me a fortune, so don't think this makes us even.'

'Now there's gratitude for you,' said Mr Toad. He turned to Ms Badger. 'My dear lady, would you do me the honour of escorting me from these woods?'

'That depends,' said Ms Badger—she held up a piece of paper, 'on whether I can add flying to this list of things you're not allowed to do.'

Mr Toad bowed his head. 'If you must.'

'Say it,' said Ms Badger.

'Very well,' said Mr Toad. 'I give you my word that I shan't fly again.'

'Or tease any more weasels,' Mo piped up.

Mr Toad gave him a stern look. 'That, my good stoat, I cannot promise.'

Ms Badger sighed. 'As long as you don't fly I suppose that'll have to do. Come on, Mr Toad, let's get you home.'

'Ooh, I nearly forgot.' Mr Toad snatched his helmet from the Chief Weasel. He tapped the camera and gave the Chief Weasel a meaningful look. 'My clever pixies. In case you decide any more trees are "unsafe".'

Ms Badger and Mr Toad walked arm in arm from the clearing. The Chief Weasel glowered at Teejay, Ratty, and Mo. 'You weasels saw nothing of this. Understood?'

They nodded, quickly.

'Now please take my daughter back to the gate. Mr Ripton and I have things to discuss.' The Chief Weasel turned away.

'Get us back to the car,' Teejay hissed to Lennie.

'Before Ms Badger gets there,' added Ratty.

'Or we're in big, big bother,' Mo finished.

Lennie grinned at them. 'Don't worry, I know all the shortcuts. She'll never even know you were gone.'

Chapter 18
The Wood Delivery

Boredy, *boredy, boredy,* wrote Teejay in her exercise book. After all her adventures Mr Polecat's lesson seemed even duller than usual.

'At least you're not hanging from a tree,' said Lennie.

'Good point,' said Teejay. 'Bored is good.'

There was a knock on the classroom door and Ms Badger walked in. 'I'm sorry to disturb you, Mr Polecat,' she said, 'but we have quite an important visitor. Can I borrow Lenora for a few minutes? Oh, and Teejay, Ratty, and Mo, you'd better come too.'

Teejay glanced at the others, then followed Ms Badger out of the school. In the playground stood Mr Toad. He beamed when he saw them.

'My friends, we are victorious,' he said.

'Those interwebby fiends have taken down that picture. They put up the film young Mole sent them instead.'

'I made a video of Mr Toad's crashes,' said Mo. 'They said it was far funnier than their website.'

'You have saved Toad Hall's reputation!'

declared Mr Toad. 'And I have been thinking about what you said, Toad Junior, about trees and suchlike. And how without dear Miss Lenora I'd still be dangling in that clearing.'

'I'm sure Daddy would have let you down,' said Lennie.

'I bet he wouldn't,' Ratty whispered. Teejay and Mo nodded.

'Nevertheless,' said Mr Toad, 'I owe you all such a debt. So I wanted to give you a little something to say thank you.'

Mr Toad disappeared around the side of the building. He came back carrying a pot containing a tiny oak tree. He presented it to Lennie.

'I know it's only small—' Mr Toad began.

Lennie squeaked. 'Oh, it's lovely!' She turned the pot in her paws. 'I'll put it straight in the clearing.'

'As I was saying,' said Mr Toad, with a wink, 'I know it's only small, so I bought a few more to keep it company.'

He led them around the corner of the school. Teejay gasped. The playing field was covered in thousands of tiny trees in bags. A fleet of lorries marked 'Great Birnam Deliveries' was waiting at the gates to be filled.

'Wow,' said Ratty, 'it's like an army of trees.'

'Mr Toad and I thought your class could plant them in the Wild Wood,' said Ms Badger. 'Lenora, could you please ask Mr Polecat to bring the rest of the class?'

Lennie rushed off to fetch the others.

Ms Badger frowned at Teejay, Ratty, and Mo. 'I'm still deciding whether I should let you lot go along. You did get Mr Toad into lots of trouble.'

'Yes, Badge.' Teejay hung her head. 'And we're really sorry.'

Ms Badger smiled, 'I know. I suppose it's not really your fault he crashed. And you did all wait for me outside the Wild Wood.'

'Well, actually—' Mo began. Ratty stepped on his foot. 'Ow! Yes, we did.'

'So given that you managed to behave for a change,' Ms Badger continued, 'I don't see why you shouldn't go too.'

'Thanks, Badge!' cried Teejay, and gave her a hug.

'Excellent, so that's settled.' Mr Toad rubbed his hands together. 'But I still say we don't need all these lorries. It would be far simpler to drop the trees from my paraglider.'

'That paraglider is off limits,' said Ms Badger.

'Then perhaps I could have a small digger?'
Ms Badger growled. 'No.'

Teejay grinned. 'Just use a spade, Mr T.'

'But is the Chief Weasel OK with us going into Wild Wood?' said Ratty.

Ms Badger chuckled. 'Oh, yes. The Chief Weasel has been very helpful, hasn't he Mr Toad?'

'He certainly has. And that nice Mr Ripton too.' Mr Toad grinned at them. 'And to think that all I had to do was say the word "pixies".'

The End. (Time to turn over a new leaf.)

The Wind in the Willows

The River Thames

Kenneth **Grahame** is the author of *The Wind in the Willows,* the book which has introduced generations of children to Mr Toad and his friends. Kenneth Grahame was born in 1859 and spent much of his childhood exploring the idyllic countryside along the banks of the River Thames and discovering its wildlife.

A water vole

Kenneth Grahame

After leaving school he began a career in the Bank of England. He married Elspeth Thomson in 1899 and they had a son, Alastair. When Alastair was about four years old, Kenneth Grahame began telling him bedtime stories that were to form the beginnings of *The Wind in the Willows*. The book was published in 1908 and has been loved by readers ever since.

Eye in the Sky

This is a recent photograph that was taken from a hot-air balloon (a form of transport that Toad himself might like to try). It shows how little the countryside in Oxfordshire and Berkshire has changed since the time when Kenneth Grahame spent happy days there boating on the river and going for woodland walks.

An aerial view of the River Thames

A note from Tom Moorhouse

Well, it was bound to happen sooner or later. Mr Toad's not the sort of amphibian to keep his feet on the ground—not when he could be up, up and away!

For a writer it was brilliant fun thinking up all the silly predicaments and terrible tangles that could befall a paragliding Toad. It was also great to explore what Teejay, Ratty and Mo were like at school (Teejay's not an ideal pupil). And it made sense to me that the weasels would also send their children there, and that the children could be friends. But the best thing about *Operation Toad!* was being able to set the action in the dark and scary Wild Wood . . . So strap in, return your seat back to the upright position, and enjoy your flight on Toad Airways. But remember: don't try to copy Mr Toad's adventures—not unless you have a Badger to rescue you!

A note from Holly Swain

I'm glad I work in a studio on my own, as often I sit here drawing, giggling to myself about amusing things I have put in my illustrations, that I hope people will find funny! There have been over 280 illustrations that I have painted for all the books in *The New Adventures of Mr Toad* series and many, many more drawings. I've used a lot of green and black paint, many pencils and piles of paper! I have

loved bringing to life the characters that Tom has written about and wondering with each new book what mischief Mr Toad will get up to, which vehicles he will destroy and how the kids will save him. This story has a bit of everything—crazy flying, spectacular falling, tears, diggers, tree chopping, weasels, disguises, friendship and hope. I hope you have enjoyed the adventures that Mr Toad, Teejay, Ratty, and Mo have had together. I certainly have!

If you'd like to read the original story, we have these editions available.

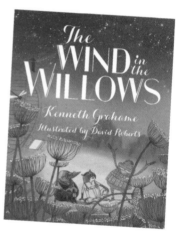